S0-CBV-208

ODYSSEY

TALES OF THE UNIVERSE

TEXT AND PHOTOGRAPHY
BY PAUL LIEBHARDT

INSTITUTE FOR SHIPBOARD EDUCATION
DESIGNED AND PRODUCED BY MICHAEL VERBOIS

Copyright © 1991 by Paul Liebhardt
All rights reserved. No part of this book may be used or reproduced in any manner
whatsoever without written permission.

ISBN 0-9628861-0-6

Published by
The Institute for Shipboard Education
811 William Pitt Union
Pittsburgh, PA 15260

Typography by
Tammy Baker Graphics

Printed in Japan by
Toppan Printing Co., Ltd.

I wish to go to latitudes where my life must become quite different to make existence possible, where understanding necessitates a radical renewal of one's means of comprehension, latitudes where I will be forced to forget that which up to now I knew and was....I want to let the climate of the tropics, the Indian mode of consciousness, the Chinese code of life and many other factors, which I cannot envisage in advance, work their spell upon me one after the other, and then watch what will become of me.

Count Keyserling

This book is dedicated to all those who have sailed on the S.S. Universe—and all those who will.

INTRODUCTION

Life at sea is indispensable, life elsewhere is not.

Plutarch

It has always been this way. The purpose of ships has been to influence, and sometimes even decide issues on land. The great seafaring peoples of the world—most notably the Greeks, the Romans, the Spanish, the English, the Germans, the Chinese, the Japanese—all have built ships that have affected the course of human events. They have been used for commerce, warfare, exploration, communication, and transportation. Historians have chronicled the life of many of these vessels. Their names are legendary: the *Queen Mary*, the *Leviathan*, the *Lusitania*, the *Empress of Japan*, the *Ile de France*, the *Calypso*, the *Mauritania*, the *Santa Maria* and of course there are so many others.

There is one ship sailing the oceans of the world today whose name is not yet widely known and whose story has yet to be told. Perhaps this is because of her unpretentious, unassuming appearance and understated style. She appears on no lists. She is not one of the twenty-five largest ships ever built, or the longest, or the fastest or most expensive. But she is unique and like all great vessels, her influence has been deep and long-lasting. Unquestionably this is because of the role she plays. Among ships she is one of a kind—the only ship in the world devoted to international education. She is the world's only floating university.

The history of this tough, old, well-traveled ocean liner, like the history of all ships, involves change, trends, and places; but most of all it involves people. Of the hundreds of individuals who have touched the life of this ship, two must be singled out as having done the most to shape her destiny.

Arnold Bernstein and C.Y. Tung could not have come from more diverse backgrounds: Bernstein, a German-Jew who served in the German army and won the Iron Cross during World War I, was born in Breslau, now a part of Poland, in 1888. Tung, a practicing Buddhist for much of his life was born in Shanghai, China, in 1912.

Despite their vastly different origins, these two men had much in common. Both came to love the sea, ships and the men who sailed them. Both became positive, dominant, headstrong entrepreneurs who built thriving shipping businesses. Both were enormously proud of the huge fleets they commanded. The funnel insignias of their ships ornamented the harbors of the world.

For C.Y. Tung it was an artistic rendition of the red Chinese plum blossom on a yellow background. For Arnold Bernstein it was the initials *AB* in the center of a white diamond on a blue and red field.

World events dictated the sea lanes these men traveled in establishing their rightful place in maritime history would be far different. There is no better illustration of this than the events of 1937, a landmark year for both men, personally and professionally.

For C.Y. Tung 1937 was a glorious year. His wife became pregnant with their first child. In his early twenties and in the employ of the Tientsin Navigation Company, he had already risen to become vice president of the Tientsin Shipowners Association. His plan for rehabilitating China's Depression-riddled shipping industry was well received by the Ministry of Transportation.

His private plans for establishing his own shipping company (formally constituted in Hong Kong as the Chinese Maritime Trust in 1941) were well underway. Late in the year Tung was transferred to the Tung Cheng Shipping Company Limited in Shanghai, a subsidiary of the Kincheng Bank. Thrust into the international banking and shipping world of Shanghai, C.Y. Tung began to develop a global vision and independent spirit that would lead to a rich and varied life.

For Arnold Bernstein 1937 was pure hell. Headquartered in Hamburg, he had risen to become president of the highly profitable Arnold Bernstein and Red Star Steamship Lines. Both were in the unique situation of being Jewish-owned shipping companies operating under the German flag with significant American financial investment (the Chemical Bank and Trust Company of New York and the Erie Railroad). In January the German Secret Police arrested Bernstein and charged him with treason and violating foreign exchange control laws. He was jailed and put on trial by the German government. Found guilty of "national treason and concealment of foreign currencies," Bernstein was sentenced as a "Nazi traitor" to thirty months in a concentration camp and fined $400,000. His property was confiscated. His shipping lines were "aryanized" and taken over by the Nazis.

Bernstein would emerge from his incarceration destitute and a broken man. But he vowed he would be a shipowner again. He wanted more than anything to help defeat the Third Reich on his own terms. It would take him years, and it would take him to a new country, but Arnold Bernstein would get his chance. In the end he would persevere and win.

Perseverance was a hallmark of C.Y. Tung's life as well. Soon after its attack on Pearl Harbor in 1941 Japan captured Hong Kong, forcing him to close his offices there. Undaunted, Tung moved the Chinese Maritime Trust to Chungking and then to Shanghai after the war. Following the Communist takeover in 1949, he fled China and moved back to Hong Kong. Despite the shortages of food and basic necessities, rampant inflation and the ravages that civil strife had caused in China, Tung set as a goal the revival of Chinese maritime greatness with ships owned, manned, operated and maintained on world routes entirely by Chinese. The success he achieved was spectacular. Eventually Tung built a fleet of liners, oil tankers and cargo carriers that would be rivaled only by those of Aristotle Onassis and Y.K. Pao.

Arnold Bernstein and C.Y. Tung would never meet. Yet it is ironic that of the hundreds of ships these two great men of shipping owned during their lifetimes, they would come to have a special affection and love for the very same ship. Both would own her—first Bernstein in 1957 and then Tung in 1971. Both would spend many happy hours roaming her decks and planning her future. Arnold Bernstein's plans were never fully realized. C.Y. Tung's were.

Known by many as the "floating university" but affectionately as "the Great White Mother" by those who know her well, this ship bears the name *S.S. Universe*. This is her story.

THE STORY OF THE UNIVERSE

She walks the waters like a thing of life,
and seems to dare the elements to strife.
Byron

Richard Burke, the president of the Sun Shipbuilding and Dry Dock Company, had a satisfied smile on his face. The date was July 1, 1953. Burke was listening attentively to a speech by Louis Rothschild, the recently appointed chairman of the Federal Maritime Board. Both men were participating in a luncheon ceremony following the launching of one of Sun's recently completed vessels.

At first she was just a number—"hull number 586." But on this bright sunny day in Chester, Pennsylvania as a bottle of champagne was smashed on her nose by her sponsor, Mrs. Robert Murray, the wife of the Under Secretary of Commerce, this vessel sprang to life. Christened the *Badger Mariner*, she had glided easily into the calm waters of the Delaware River.

None of the dignitaries attending the luncheon could have known how influential the *Badger Mariner* would become in the lives of so many young college students in the future. What they did know for certain was that they were participating in the first American maritime mobilization program since the end of World War II. It was a program that produced the thirty-five fastest, most powerful and, in terms of dead-weight tonnage, largest cargo vessels ever to fly the American flag. Each bearing the nickname of a different state, they were known as the *Mariners*.

In the summer of 1950, only five years after the surrender of the Germans and the Japanese brought an end to World War II, another bitter armed conflict dominated the headlines of the world's newspapers. On the 24th of August, North Koreans crossed the 38th Parallel, precipitating the Korean War. With the sudden return of American fighting men to combat, the Military Sea Transportation Service was confronted with an urgent requirement for ships.

Almost as soon as Korean hostilities began military authorities turned to privately owned shipping lines for the use of all available tonnage. It did not take long for America's private merchant ships to be absorbed. Meanwhile, the Military Sea Transportation Service requested the Maritime Administration to withdraw from its national defense reserve fleet the best of the ships then in lay-up.

The ships most serviceable were the one hundred or so remaining fifteen-knot *Victory* class cargo ships that were built during the later part of World War II. Most of the *Victories* were quickly repaired, outfitted, and put into service. All that remained in the reserve fleet anchorages were about 1,200 of the old, slow, ten-knot *Liberty* ships, the workhorses of World War II.

The age and slow speed of the vessels in the reserve fleet presented a bleak picture to Vice Admiral E.L. Cochrane when he assumed office as Maritime Administrator in August 1950. Only a short time earlier he had served with a team of engineers assigned to determine what kind of ship could best strengthen the United States national defense and at the same time compete with the best modern ships of foreign nations in international trade.

The team had settled on the concept of a fast and large cargo vessel, which could be used with the maximum guarantee of safety in transporting a steady flow of vital cargoes and manpower into forward war areas. Because of rapid advances made during World War II in undersea and air attack techniques, it was decided the ship must be capable of high speed and run independently of convoys if need be. Using the team's concept as a guide, Cochrane began preparing the preliminary design for a high speed cargo ship that would modernize the American Merchant Marine fleet.

While the design work was going forward, appropriate members of Congress were made aware of the critical need for the new ship. House and Senate concern, coupled with President Truman's declaration of a national emergency in December, precipitated one of the first actions of the new Congress: on January 3, 1951, a $350 million authorization to the Maritime Administration for a shipbuilding program as part of the national mobilization effort.

Invitations to bid for the construction of the new ship were issued January 10, 1951. By July contracts had been awarded to seven shipyards—five on the east coast, one on the Gulf coast, and one on the Pacific coast. Each yard was to build five ships.

Spreading the work out across the United States was done for defense as well as economic reasons. The average contract price for each ship was $8,441,332.

Once production of these new vessels was underway, Cochrane selected the class name *Mariner* as descriptive and appropriate for a ship whose "trim, yacht-like lines truly symbolized the new forward look of the American Merchant Marine."

Each of the thirty-five ships had to meet five design criteria:

- The ships had to be economically sound, i.e. potentially profitable to shipowners and operators in peacetime, as well as specially tailored for the needs of war. Simply put, this meant the design had to meet both the requirements of an all-purpose commercial carrier and a naval auxiliary ship without destroying the usefulness of either.
- Speed and maneuverability was paramount. The ships needed enough speed to be able to outrun the fastest Russian submarines.
- It had to be possible to convert the ship with a minimum of effort for service as a transport, supply ship, or even a passenger ship. A variety of cargoes and trade routes had to be considered.
- Special attention had to be given to cargo handling systems maximizing the ship's efficiency and minimizing time spent in port.
- "Critical" materials had to be avoided in order to facilitate construction of additional *Mariners,* even under conditions of increased hostilities.

Named for the state of Wisconsin, the *Badger Mariner* was the twenty-second *Mariner* to be launched. In sea trials the new ship surpassed all expectations of speed and performance. Her main engine, a geared turbine, drove a twenty two foot-diameter propeller, giving her a speed of twenty knots at 175,500 shaft horsepower.

The *Badger Mariner,* like her *Mariner* sisters, had a deckhouse amidships providing accommodations for twelve passengers and a crew of fifty-eight officers and men, space for the wheel house and navigating and radio equipment.

Her hull form (developed by the Bethlehem Steel Company and used on all the *Mariners*) had a main and second deck that extended the length of the ship. A third deck fitted below the second deck and extended part way from the bow aft.

The *Badger* was divided by nine watertight transverse bulkheads carried up to the main deck. She had a double bottom that was subdivided into tanks for fuel oil and ballast. She had seven cargo holds, four forward and three aft of the machinery spaces, and provisions were made for carrying refrigerated as well as dry and liquid cargo.

The new *Mariner* fleet compiled a distinguished service record. By April 1954 *Mariners* had tramped nearly 1.5 million miles in practically every ocean of the world. They carried cargoes that ranged from an entire cement plant to latex to oil reactors and weapons. Only one *Mariner* was lost. Nebraska's namesake, the *Cornhusker,* was wrecked on Oryok To, just off Pusan, Korea in 1953.

The *Badger's* own record was routine. On October 29, 1953 she was assigned to the South Atlantic Steamship Line for government acceptance. She made only one eighty-nine day voyage covering 24,000 miles. On June 10, 1954 she was reassigned to the Maritime Administration's National Defense Reserve Fleet in the Hudson River.

1954 was a pivotal year for the remaining thirty-four *Mariners.* Once a truce between North and South Korea was signed in June 1953, the Maritime Administration began selling the *Mariners* to American flag steamship operators and there was a rush to buy them. The price set by Congress (around $5 million each) made them among the great bargains of maritime history. George Killian, president of the American President Lines, alone purchased and converted eight *Mariners* characterizing his investment as "one of the most progressive steps APL had ever taken" and calling the *Mariners* "the most modern cargo carriers afloat."

By December 1956, the Maritime Administration had disposed of all the *Mariners* except one. Twenty-eight were in, or about to be put in, private service and five were in use as naval auxiliaries. The only remaining *Mariner* was moored at an anchorage off Jones Point in the Hudson River. However, the Maritime Administration had plans for the *Badger Mariner.*

S.S. Badger Mariner 1953

Maritime officials had long wanted to increase American flag passenger service on the North Atlantic. They had another, less well publicized desire for a passenger/cargo vessel that could increase America's troop-lift capability during an emergency. On December 13, 1956 an invitation was issued by the Maritime Administration asking American flag steamship operators to submit bids for the purchase of the *Badger Mariner.* The invitation for bids contained several stipulations:

- The minimum bid the government would accept was $4,730,745.
- The bidder had to agree to convert the *Badger* to a combination passenger/cargo ship to be operated on "essential foreign trade route 8" (U.S. North Atlantic route to Belgium and the Netherlands).
- The bidder had to agree to expend not less than $10 million for the conversion work.

- The bidder had to agree to build a second vessel at a later date which would be put into service with the converted *Badger*.

Results of the bidding were announced January 4, 1957. It didn't take long. There was only one bidder, and the bid was for precisely $4,730,745. The Maritime Administration was pleased the bid came from someone it knew—someone with extensive experience in transporting people as well as cargo across the Atlantic—someone who had pioneered tourist-class transatlantic travel in 1933 with a $145 Hamburg-New York fare. He was a man who conceived the idea of redesigning the interior of ships so they could handle large numbers of unboxed automobiles. With two rapidly growing fleets at his command and well on his way to building a vast mercantile empire, he was the central figure in the North Atlantic steamship field in the 1930s. The man's name was Arnold Bernstein.

Arnold Bernstein

After two-and-a-half years in a concentration camp and the payment of a $30,000 ransom by some American friends, Bernstein "escaped" to the United States. When he arrived in New York on September 1, 1939 aboard the Holland America liner *Nieu Amsterdam*, Bernstein was fifty-one-years-old and penniless. The dockside interview he gave was telling:

I once employed thousands of men. In 1935 I brought the Red Star Lines under the German flag and hired 600 more seamen. But I was a Jew and the Germans couldn't have me entering in conversations with the Reich leaders. They had to get rid of me. And they did it.

It wasn't long after becoming an American citizen that Bernstein was back on his feet and again active in the shipping business. He became a predominant figure in the coal chartering field and during World War II operated government-owned vessels. After the war he wanted desperately to operate a tourist-class passenger vessel; but that opportunity was denied him when the Korean conflict made it impossible for him to obtain ships from the government for passenger conversion. Now, he felt certain, after a long and stormy career in shipping, the *Badger Mariner* was the answer to his prayers.

Once Bernstein had her, life took on an accelerated pace for the *Badger*. With a Maritime Administration construction and operating subsidy in his pocket, he took her to Pascagoula, Mississippi, where, at a cost of $11 million the Ingalls Shipbuilding Corporation would do the conversion.

Together with his financial backer, The American Securities Corporation, Bernstein formed a new shipping line to operate the ship. He named it the American Banner Line, assuring that the initials *AB* would still be displayed prominently on the new ship. The line was admitted to membership in the Transatlantic Passenger Conference, which set a minimum off-season rate of $186.50 for a crossing. A year-round schedule of seven-day crossings between New York and Europe was planned. Bernstein was named president of the line and Vice Admiral Roscoe Hillenkoetter, a former CIA director, was named Executive Vice President. Hillenkoetter summed up the philosophy of the new line his first day on the job:

American Banner Lines plans to provide distinctive accommodations attractive to the American tourist, and with conveniences that the people of this country expect. This is to be done at the lowest practicable cost. I believe that such a program will stimulate increased travel, and such travel should lead to more friendly understanding, first among individuals, and ultimately among nations.

It was a philosophy that would always remain with this ship.

On June 5, 1957 Bernstein named his new ship the *S.S. Atlantic*. Exactly one year later to the day, on June 5, 1958, the *Atlantic* entered her new home port—the Port of New York for the first time. Heralded by the press as America's newest "sea queen" and a United States "challenger" to European dominance of the North Atlantic low-cost tourist trade, she was given the traditional welcome accorded vessels making their first visit to the harbor. Crowds cheered, helicopters whirled overhead, harborcraft tooted, fireboats sprayed and Nat Fein, the New York Herald Tribune's Pulitzer Prize-winning photographer, snapped pictures as the *Atlantic* made her way through the Narrows and into the East River.

As she first loomed into view early in the afternoon, Bernstein exclaimed to a welcoming party aboard the tugboat *Dalzellerta*: "Look, look—she's beautiful. What lines she's got." And almost breathlessly he murmured to himself, "Today I am reborn."

If Bernstein was reborn, the *Badger* was too. She looked nothing like her former *Mariner* self. From a ship that had been designed to carry less than one hundred people, she had been transformed into one that could carry well over 1,000. Within her freshly painted black hull and new white superstructure were accommodations for 320 crew members and 900 passengers—forty in first class and 860 in tourist class.

American Banner had a lot to brag about their one and only ship. The *Atlantic* was completely air conditioned. Every cabin had wall-to-wall carpeting and a private bathroom with a shower stall. All the rooms were located amidships "where the riding is gentlest."

But what pleased Bernstein most was that the *S.S. Atlantic* was the first U.S.-flag liner to be almost entirely tourist class. Except for the forty berths and small adjacent dining hall and lounge on boat deck reserved for first class, the tourist class passengers had the run of the ship. It was "passenger freedom" in which Bernstein took personal pride: "On this ship the tourist passenger will have dignity—he won't have anybody looking down on him. It will be his ship...every passenger will be able to enjoy the 600-foot glass-enclosed promenade deck as well as the freedom of the sports and sun deck, lounges, night clubs and bar." There would be no snobbery on Bernstein's *Atlantic*. It would be a characteristic, like Hillenkoetter's philosophy, that would always remain with this ship.

Perhaps the most unusual feature Bernstein incorporated on the *Atlantic* was what he called "the electronic babysitter." Thirty-five staterooms were equipped with an audio system connected to a monitor board in the ship's hospital. By flicking a switch as they left their rooms, parents would be assured that any wail of distress their child might make would be picked up by a microphone and transmitted to a nurse on duty. A trained attendant would then be dispatched to the designated room.

Arnold Bernstein had often said that on the day that the *Atlantic* sailed from New York to Zeebrugge, Belgium and Amsterdam, Holland he would have "defeated Hitler." June 11, 1958 was that day.

The ship was completely sold out, but the *S.S. Atlantic's* maiden voyage did not get off to a smooth start. First, its departure from the Kent Street, Brooklyn pier was delayed almost an hour because her 900 passengers had to lug their own luggage aboard—union pickets, who were disputing American Banner's hiring practices, kept longshoremen off the pier. Although some crew members pitched in to help passengers and the longshoremen eventually consented to loading the mail, it was a chaotic few hours. To make matters worse an anonymous call set off a bomb scare that brought two police launches, a Coast Guard cutter and a car full of policemen to the pier.

The *Atlantic's* first master, Captain Aime Gerber, had other problems: He had to undock his ship without the aid of tugs because the tugboatmen were honoring the picket lines. He was then forced to take his new ship to an anchorage just below the Statue of Liberty where she spent a long afternoon waiting for the arrival of special launches carrying thirteen crew members and two passengers who had missed the ship's departure. At 5:15 she was finally able to head out to the ocean that was her namesake.

It was an inauspicious start for the *Atlantic* and the new era of American-flag transatlantic travel that she had inaugurated on this day. Perhaps, however, the obstacles she overcame in the first hours of her maiden voyage toughened her and helped prepare her for the sometimes rough seas she would encounter in the years ahead.

One year later, on a hot June day in New York, the *Atlantic* celebrated her first birthday as the flagship for American Banner. No one knew it then, but it would be her last. The ceremonies at Pier 97 on West 57th Street were upbeat. The *Atlantic's* second master, Captain Konstanty Kowalski sliced a birthday cake while Admiral Hillenkoetter declared that the *Atlantic* had won gratifying response from the traveling public. She had completed twenty roundtrips across the Atlantic. But there would only be a few more. On November 3, 1959 Arnold Bernstein sadly announced the discontinuance of his sixteen month-old service. He had had his revenge on Hitler, but time had passed him by: In October 1958, just four

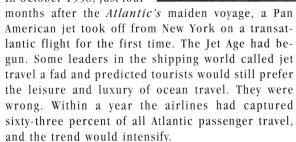

*S.S. Atlantic
American Banner
Lines, 1958*

months after the *Atlantic's* maiden voyage, a Pan American jet took off from New York on a transatlantic flight for the first time. The Jet Age had begun. Some leaders in the shipping world called jet travel a fad and predicted tourists would still prefer the leisure and luxury of ocean travel. They were wrong. Within a year the airlines had captured sixty-three percent of all Atlantic passenger travel, and the trend would intensify.

But it was not only just the jet airplane that caused the collapse of American Banner. There were three other factors.

First, the *Atlantic* was allowed to serve only a limited number of European ports. By the terms of Bernstein's subsidy agreement with the government, American Banner could call only on Zeebrugge and Amsterdam. In May 1959 he applied for a revision of his permit so the ship could serve Southampton,

England, the most popular destination for transatlantic ship passengers. But his request was denied.

Second, Bernstein was never able to obtain a running mate for the *Atlantic*. No federal funds to assist construction of a second ship were available. And since passenger bookings were steadily declining, Bernstein's creditors were not disposed to fund another ship.

Finally, the *Atlantic* had been found to need stabilizers, which Bernstein and his backers, already heavily mortgaged, could not afford.

The *Atlantic* made her last voyage from Amsterdam to New York on October 25, 1959, less than seventeen months after her rebirth in that same port. Only 353 passengers were on board. Bernstein then laid up the ship he cared for so much at the Bethlehem Steel yard in Hoboken, New Jersey. Yet, as it turned out, the *Atlantic's* life as an ocean liner was just beginning.

For Arnold Bernstein the *Atlantic* represented a climax. Her lay-up would mark the end of his four decades in shipping. He retired, became interested in ecology and wrote extensively on the subject. He was engrossed in writing his memoirs when he died in March 1971. He was eighty-three.

Admiral John Will, president of the American Export Lines, already had twin twenty-six-knot luxury liners in his fleet. But he felt these ships, the *Independence* and the *Constitution*, needed a sister ship to enable his line to maintain a schedule of frequent sailings to the Mediterranean and the Middle East. It was a route that he felt was growing and important. The less luxurious *Atlantic*, he thought, would round-out his fleet perfectly.

S.S. Atlantic
American Export
Lines, 1960

In early February 1960, the Maritime Administration approved sale of the *Atlantic* to the American Export Lines. A $2 million improvement program was begun immediately. The *Atlantic* was taken back to where life began for her, the Sun Shipbuilding and Dry Dock Company of Chester, Pennsylvania. There, in just forty-nine working days, major changes were made.

A 25-by-30-foot swimming pool was installed on the upper deck. At the time it was the largest outdoor pool on any transatlantic liner. The play deck around the pool was enlarged, sheeted with wood decking, and fitted with tables and umbrellas.

The *Atlantic's* hull was painted white and the ship's single stack was painted to match those on the *Independence* and *Constitution*.

A 41 by 85 foot steel and glass enclosed solarium was constructed on the sun deck and fitted for recreational activities. A new fireproof projection booth permitted the showing of first-run Cinemascope movies to passengers.

Also added was a new laundry, steel kennels to accommodate pets, additional passenger service pantries, more bathrooms adjoining the public areas around the ship, a new elevator to expedite baggage handling, and space to accommodate passenger automobiles was increased substantially.

Sun's refurbishing did nothing to change the overall character of the *S.S. Atlantic*. She retained the informal style that passengers had come to love. She remained the furthest thing from the classic European luxury liner. New York Port authorities, however, recognized the importance of the *Atlantic* to American commerce and did something unique on her maiden American Export voyage: As she eased into the Hudson River on May 16, 1960, the *Atlantic* was given a traditional "port welcome" ordinarily reserved for incoming ships, the first time in maritime history that the procedure had been reversed. Ships and harborcraft saluted her as she sailed down the Hudson. When she passed the Battery, fireboats shot streams of water skyward while a parade of tugs, with all signal flags flying, blasted a greeting to the Mediterranean-bound liner.

In further tribute, arrangements were made for the master of the *S.S. Atlantic* to broadcast a radio message from the bridge at sailing time. The message was heard by dockside officials participating in the pre-sailing ceremonies and broadcast live throughout the city over radio station WNYC:

This is Captain Leif J. Christiansen, master of the 18,000 ton U.S.-flag liner S.S. Atlantic. We have just cast off the lines at Pier 84 to begin our maiden voyage in American Export Lines' Sunlane Service between New York and Spain, Greece, and Israel. The Atlantic will sail regularly in this service each month.

The Atlantic...is the only U.S.-flag tourist-class ship in transatlantic service. As such, it will have an important mission to strengthen our nation's trade ties with friendly nations abroad.

My congratulations to the City of New York for its interest in calling public attention to the importance of American ocean shipping; its value to American business, agriculture and industry in the development of world trade and to the indispensable role of the American Merchant Marine in support of the national defense.

The *Atlantic* proved to be a workhorse for American Export Lines. Soon her Mediterranean Sunlane Service would expand: The *Atlantic* became a familiar sight in harbors in Morocco, France, Gibraltar, and the Azores. During the winter months the Meyer Davis Orchestra played calypso as the *Atlantic* was placed in service in the Caribbean. Called "Beachcomber Cruises," she made frequent calls at Jamaica, Haiti, Puerto Rico, and the Virgin Islands.

By mid-1965 the *Atlantic* had made eighty-one voyages for American Export. Anti-roll stabilizing fins had been added and a kosher kitchen as well. The *Atlantic* had now become a totally "one-class ship." The space that had been set aside for forty first-class passengers had been eliminated. American Export Lines launched a massive advertising campaign keyed to the new "one-class" character of the ship, but it had only moderate effect. There was no doubt that the jet airliner was winning the battle of the Atlantic. By mid-1966 American Export began to face hard economic realities. Fewer and fewer people were crossing the Atlantic by ship, more and more by plane. And a new challenger was on its way—the Boeing 747.

In an effort to keep her sailing profitably, the *Atlantic* was assigned a new home port—Port Everglades, Florida. This pleased Hayden Burns, the governor of the state. He remembered well how the *Atlantic* had made history in 1960 when she became the first U.S. flag passenger liner to begin a transatlantic sailing from Florida. So he welcomed her back noting that many of the seventeen million tourists who yearly visit his state would be delighted to have increased service to the Caribbean. With the transatlantic passenger market all but lost to the jetliner, American Export hoped to cash in on the growing market for Caribbean cruises.

It was all to no avail. In addition to the jet plane, American Export fell victim to rising operating costs and competition from foreign-flag cruise ships with cheaper labor. To make matters worse, the *Atlantic* suffered some negative publicity in June 1967 when she strayed out of her Port Everglades channel and ran aground in nineteen feet of water. There was no significant damage to the ship and there were no injuries; but 315 passengers were stranded for forty-eight hours.

American Export withdrew the *Atlantic* from service and laid her up in Brooklyn October 13, 1967. In the spring of 1968 one last-ditch effort was made to keep her out of mothballs. Plans were drawn up by American Export together with the Diners/Fugazy Corporation to convert the *Atlantic* into what would be called the "American World Trade Ship."

The *Atlantic* was to be altered to become a worldwide display case for American products. The ship was to be redesigned to provide exhibit space for over 300 American manufacturers. Units of exhibit space ranging from sixteen square feet to 3,000 square feet would be offered at a minimum cost to a manufacturer of $600 per port visited. The ship would also have facilities for passengers, sales meetings, and conferences. The tentative plan was for the *Atlantic* to make her first cruise to fifty-five major foreign ports in early 1969, and its message when it sailed the world would be simple: "Buy American."

Vice President Hubert Humphrey and the National Maritime Union endorsed the project as a unique and positive plan for expanding American exports. But the plan bogged down in red tape. The Maritime Administration, whose approval was required before the ship could be altered, never gave the project its blessing. Late in 1968 the plan was scrapped.

Losing this opportunity to sail the *Atlantic* again was a major disappointment to American Export. Equally disappointing were the 1968 travel statistics: Transatlantic passenger ships handled only seven percent or 394,000 of the 5,633,000 passengers on the route. The *Atlantic*'s days as a liner seemed to be over. American Export moved her to Baltimore March 14, 1969, where it was cheaper to keep her than anywhere else.

To the occasional passerby who observed the once proud vessel floating lifelessly at an obscure pier in Baltimore, it must have been a dismal sight. No one could have predicted the glory years of this ship were still ahead, except maybe one man. His name was C.Y. Tung of Hong Kong.

Tung purchased the *Atlantic* from American Export in the summer of 1971 for a paltry $2.4 million. It must have seemed like a bargain to him considering close to $25 million in construction and conversion costs had been invested in her. But C.Y. Tung was not just out bargain hunting in the summer of 1971. His reasons for buying the *Atlantic* and the role he eventually carved out for her related more to the kind of shipowner he was and to his own personal beliefs as a man.

Tung would eventually become the world's leading independent shipowner, commanding a fleet of over 150 ships totaling more than eleven million tons.

But unlike his Greek shipping titan counterparts Aristotle Onassis and Stavros Livanos, who lived swashbuckling and ostentations lives, C.Y. Tung was an ascetic.

He was a short, soft-spoken man who neither smoked nor drank, owned no yachts, race horses, private planes or Rolls Royces. He led a simple life, but it was a life filled with accomplishment, not only in shipping, but in international banking, insurance, film making, the arts and, ultimately, the field of education.

C.Y. Tung always had a deep and abiding respect for learning and scholarship. It was, no doubt, his Chinese heritage that made him recognize that all things were related, and in the constant quest for understanding among nations every available resource had to be used, even ships. The *S.S. Atlantic* would be C.Y. Tung's special contribution to this quest.

C.Y. Tung

"I have learned there is a link between ships and education," he was fond of saying. "They can be used for carrying ideas as well as cargo." The sequence of events that would lead to the *Atlantic's* role as a ship for "carrying ideas" really began in 1965 while she was still transporting passengers across the Atlantic. It was in that year that a small liberal arts school in Southern California called Chapman College began a unique program in international education that came to be known as World Campus Afloat.

Using a ship supplied by the Holland America Line, twice a year the college administered 110-day academic voyages around the world. In effect, Chapman College created a fully functioning university on board a ship. Students from colleges and universities across America enrolled, earned college credits that could be transferred to their home institution, and traveled the world. World Campus Afloat was not a new concept. The idea of a floating university can be traced to the experimental university voyages run by Dean James Edwin Lough of New York University in the mid-1920s. There were a few other attempts to establish similar programs in America after World War II. All of them failed—problems of finances, academic soundness and recruitment seemed insurmountable.

Little Chapman College, however, was having great success. By spring of 1970 they had run seven voyages. With each succeeding one the program gained national popularity with students and credibility within the academic community. It was in 1970 that the Holland America Line gave Chapman some bad news. The ship it was using, the 15,000-ton *S.S. Ryndam*, was in need of a major overhaul. The costs for the work were estimated at between $2 and $4 million. The shipping line refused to finance the needed work; Chapman college could not afford it. If the World Campus Afloat program was to survive, a new ship would have to be found.

When C.Y. Tung heard of Chapman's problem he offered a spectacular solution. It was a solution that stunned not only World Campus Afloat officials, but the entire shipping world. C.Y. Tung had purchased the largest passenger liner ever built—the onetime pride of the Cunard Line, the *RMS Queen Elizabeth*. Tung promised Chapman he would make appropriate modifications to this former first lady of the sea and have her ready for the fall 1971 sailing of World Campus Afloat. Tragically, it was a promise he would not be able to keep.

The *Queen Elizabeth* was taken out of service by Cunard in 1967, the same year that American Export removed the *Atlantic*. Cunard's terse announcement vividly made clear the facts of transatlantic travel: "We do not intend to operate passenger ships just because they exist." It was the end of a glorious career: heroism as a troop carrier ferrying nearly a million GI's to and from Europe in World War II, and grandeur as the most luxurious ship afloat when the war was over. For more than twenty years tycoons and dowagers would stride her polished decks, lovers danced the fox trot, and tuxedos and formals were standard at dinner. Above all this 84,000-ton, twelve-decked liner had dignity. But when C.Y. Tung found her the dignity was gone. She lay laced to the land, floating heavily in the motionless waters of a cutoff near the intercoastal waterway in Fort Lauderdale, Florida. She was also sinking quickly in a sea of red ink.

Cunard sold the *Queen* in 1968 to a group of Philadelphia businessmen who took her to Fort Lauderdale to become a tourist attraction. Guided tours of the ship were first offered in February 1969; a year later the venture was losing money at the rate of $20,000 a month. The owners declared bankruptcy and the *Queen* was placed in receivership. On September 10, 1970 the once majestic super-liner would suffer the ignominious fate of being sold at public auction.

There was electricity in the air in and around the Fort Lauderdale Galt Ocean Mile Hotel, the site of the auction. Rumors were rampant as to who the bidders would be. Some said Howard Hughes, others Onassis. There was speculation that an investment group wanted the *Queen* to serve as an off-shore arena for a heavyweight championship fight between Mohammed Ali and Joe Frazier. Most thought wealthy Italian scrap dealers had the inside track. They were all wrong. Within three minutes of the opening of the bidding C.Y. Tung had submitted the successful bid of $3.2 million.

Tung renamed the *Queen* the *S.S. Seawise University* ("Seawise" being a play on his initials, C.Y.) and together with Chapman College began making elaborate plans for her to replace the *Ryndam*. The plans called for the World Campus Afloat program to be expanded in order to permit other accredited institutions to participate. Universities around the world would be encouraged to add programs tailored to shipboard education. Classroom space and living accommodations were being planned to handle as many as 1,800 students.

While Tung was finalizing plans with Chapman he became aware of Secretary General U Thant's proposal to the General Assembly that serious thought be given to the establishment of a United Nations University. Thant wanted a university that would be "truly international in character and devoted to the Charter objectives of peace and progress." The idea intrigued Tung. He contacted Thant, offered his support, and suggested that at some point in the future the *Seawise* might be the appropriate setting for such a university. For now, however, the *Seawise* would be Chapman's.

In order to make the old *Queen* ready for her 1971 debut as a floating university, Tung planned to sail her to Hong Kong for a $5 million overhaul. But first, a major effort was required to make the *Queen* seaworthy. Thirty years of hard service, a war, and three and a half million miles followed by two years of neglect and languishing in the Florida sun had taken a toll. The *Queen's* engines and boilers needed major repair. Without varnish her decks had begun to rot, and the steel plates of her hull were rusting away at the rate of an estimated quarter of an inch a year. Tung flew in Morley Cho, one of his business associates, and William Hsuan and T.K. Yip, two of his senior captains, to take charge of his new vessel. Hsuan was named the *Seawise University's* first captain. He would be at the helm when she sailed for Hong Kong five months later.

After the installation of close to $1 million worth of spare parts flown in from England, and a number of postponements because of boiler problems, a rusty and weary looking *Seawise University* finally left her Florida dock at 8:55 a.m. February 10, 1971. It was to be a forty-five-day voyage to Hong Kong, with calls at Capetown and Singapore for bunkers. Only six of her twelve boilers were

operative, and she was expected to travel only on two of her four screws at fifteen knots. Standing next to Hsuan on the bridge as the *Seawise* threaded her way through the narrow neck of the Port Everglades inlet, was the old *Queen's* last skipper, Commodore Geoffrey Marr. He was sailing in an advisory capacity and planning to write his memoirs during the voyage. A single blast from her whistle signaled her arrival in the Atlantic. Crowds of onlookers on the south jetty of the cut cheered and honked the horns of their cars in response. The first voyage of the *Seawise University* had begun. Fate dictated it would be her last.

For the 300 Chinese nationals and 16 Britons serving as crew, the *Seawise University* became the proverbial "slow-boat to China." Before the Fort Lauderdale harbor pilot even was off the ship, one of her boilers blew. Five days later the *Seawise* lost power completely while she was in the windward passage. The giant 1,031 foot liner drifted helplessly until the tug *Rescue* arrived the next day and tried to tow the dead ship to Jamaica. The *Rescue* made practically no headway; the load was simply too much. The Dutch salvage tug *Jacob Van Heemskerck* was then called in to assist. It took the two tugs eight days to get the *Seawise* to an anchorage off Oranjestad, Aruba. She would remain there for almost two months.

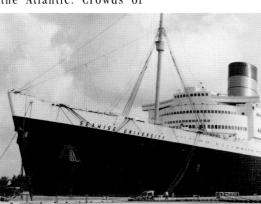

S.S. Seawise University, Fort Lauderdale, Florida, 1970

A close examination of the *Seawise University* determined that strong leaks had developed in four of her five operating boilers. The repair work required that technicians and parts be flown in from Hong Kong. It would be a difficult two months, requiring some drastic measures: An acute water shortage necessitated gravity activated latrines to be suspended over the side of the ship. Finally, repairs complete, the *Seawise* resumed her trip to Hong Kong on May 8. She steamed at a reduced working pressure of 360 pounds to lessen the load on her boilers. After stops in Curacao, Singapore and Capetown the "Old Queen" (sarcastically dubbed "Limp-a-Long Liz" by the press) made port in Hong Kong July 16. A gala banquet on the ship that evening celebrated her safe arrival, yet the respite was brief for the old ship and her crew. The next morning workmen began the massive job of converting the *Seawise* to a university.

For C.Y. Tung it was time of mixed emotions: joy at knowing that he had kept a famous vessel off the scrap heap and that the noble cause of international education lay ahead. But Tung was disappointed, too, that the *Seawise's* six-month delay would not enable him to keep his promise to Chapman College of a fall 1971 sailing of World Campus Afloat. It was at this juncture that Tung decided to buy the *Atlantic* and offer her to Chapman College to serve as a temporary replacement for the *Seawise University.* His

The Seawise fire, Hong Kong Harbor, January 9, 1972

decision would have a profound impact not only on World Campus Afloat, but also on American shipboard education in general as it would progress through the 1980s and 1990s. The *S.S. Atlantic* turned out to be not a temporary replacement for the *Seawise,* but a permanent one. The old *Queen Elizabeth* would never leave Hong Kong Harbor.

As the conversion work on the *Seawise* commenced in earnest, in another harbor half way across the world there was a flurry of activity on board the *Atlantic.* A team of technicians had been flown to Baltimore from Taiwan to get the ship, idle now for four years, ready to sail again. Chinese know-how, teamwork and dedication brought the *Atlantic* in a few short months back to operating condition.

Tung renamed his new ship the *S.S. Universe Campus,* registered her in Liberia and made her part of his Orient Overseas Line. She was serving only as "a substitute for a Queen," but when the *Universe Campus* departed Los Angeles on September 1, 1971 with nearly 400 eager college students on board, it marked the beginning of a brand new chapter in the life of the *Atlantic.* For the first time she sailed under a foreign flag; she had a Chinese captain and crew, and a cargo unlike any she had ever carried.

The *Universe Campus* completed her first around-the-world voyage as a floating university when she sailed back into her old home port of New York on December 23, 1971. Pipes had leaked, drenching cabins and classrooms; air conditioning failed. Yet Dr. Desmond Bittinger and Captain Koo, the *Universe Campus'* first Dean and first Master, respectively, pronounced the voyage an overwhelming success. As students and faculty disembarked on that chilly December day in New York, they spoke in glowing terms about the ship they had come to know so well. They had affectionately nicknamed her "The Great White Mother," a name that would stick with her forever.

Chapman's planning for the spring 1972 World Campus Afloat voyage to Africa, India, the Orient, and Japan was well underway. With 450 students and a faculty and staff of 65 signed up for the February 3 sailing, preparations on the *Universe Campus* began almost immediately.

Meanwhile preparations of a different kind were taking place on the *Seawise University.* A farewell cocktail party was to be given for the men who had worked so diligently on the conversion. By January 1972, after an expenditure of nearly $6 million, the *Seawise* was ready to sail to Japan for dry docking.

On the morning of January 9, the day before the sailing, some 2,000 workmen and their families were on board sightseeing. Many were to take part in the cocktail party planned for later in the afternoon. The party never took place. At about 10:30 a.m., fire seemed to erupt everywhere at once and spread with lightning speed throughout the ship. A helicopter pilot reported the blaze to harbor officials about midday.

Eighty percent of the superstructure was ablaze when fireboats and fire engines mounted on ferry boats arrived on the scene. Some 200 workmen had to jump for their lives into the harbor or climb down anchor chains and ropes. The fire was fed by a diesel oil tank that had exploded, and strong winds helped spread the flames. By early evening the inferno lit up Hong Kong harbor in one of the most spectacular and disastrous waterfront fires ever witnessed. About eight hours after the fire began, the giant vessel listed seventeen degrees to starboard as the entire superstructure became enveloped in flames. The "Old Queen" burned fiercely throughout the night and on into the following morning.

As the sun rose, the fire appeared to diminish except for an occasional burst of flames near the bow. At about noon the mighty ship finally gave up, turned over, and sank in forty-three feet of water. The former queen of the Atlantic lay on her side, her one remaining funnel just visible above the water line. Commented one harbor official, "She just rolled over and died."

A shocked and grieving C.Y. Tung left London January 10 to inspect the wreckage. He offered a brief and emotional statement to the press as he left Britain: "I feel so bad. It is the only historical ship left. We restored her to her former glory. It makes me cry but I must be strong in my nerve."

Tung did remain strong in his nerve. Although the *Queen* was dead, his commitment to providing a ship to support the cause of international education was unwavering.

The ten-year period following the tragedy in Hong Kong Harbor would bring a number of changes to shipboard education in America. Though it all Tung and his ship played a dominant role. In 1975, after four years and eight globe-circling voyages by the *Universe Campus*, financial problems at Chapman forced it to give up its World Campus Afloat program. C.Y. Tung wanted to find a way to keep the *Universe Campus* sailing as a floating university. So did two officials of the World Campus Afloat program who had helped make the program grow into an exciting educational option for American college students. Dr. Merwin Griffiths and Dr. John Tymitz left Chapman and with the support and financial backing of C.Y. Tung formed a non-profit educational corporation headquartered in Laguna Hills, California called the Institute for Shipboard Education.

It took the newly formed institute about a year and a half to canvas potential academic sponsors, develop its own plans for the *Universe Campus* and publicize them to the academic community. During this period Tung used the ship to run cruises from Los Angeles to the west coast of Mexico and through the Panama Canal to the Caribbean. To make the ship appear more palatable to "cruise-type" passengers, in 1976 Tung dropped the word "campus" from her name. She would henceforth be known simply as the *S.S. Universe*.

In 1976 the Institute for Shipboard Education entered into an agreement with the University of Colorado at Boulder to establish the academic program—approve faculty, establish curriculum, register students, issue transcripts, etc.—on board the *Universe*. Griffiths and Tymitz chose the name "Semester at Sea" for America's newest and boldest program of college-level education.

Ironically, at the same time that C.Y. Tung was preparing for the inaugural voyage of Semester at Sea on the *S.S. Universe*, curious visitors were still touring Hong Kong harbor in colorful junks that would invariably stop at a black hulk that rose about fifteen feet out of the water. A few hundred feet of charred steel was all that was left to see of the *Seawise University*. Only the mid-section of its blackened, twisted structure peaked above the sea. Slowly but surely divers and explosive experts had been chipping away at the bow and stern. The metal was being sold as scrap throughout Asia. Many of the maritime historians who stopped to gaze at the remains of this onetime monarch of the seas could not help but recall the words of Queen Elizabeth (now Queen mother) as she spoke in Clydebank, Scotland at the September 27, 1938 launching of the ship that bore her name:

We proclaim our belief that by the grace of God and by man's patience and goodwill, order may yet be brought out of confusion and peace out of turmoil. With that hope and prayer in our hearts we send forth upon her mission this noble ship.

The words would have applied equally well on February 25, 1977, when the *S.S. Universe* departed Los Angeles on her maiden Semester at Sea voyage. Left in her wake was a period of great instability and unrest in American society—political assassinations, the civil rights struggle, Woodstock, Vietnam, and Watergate. It was a time when college students everywhere were anxious to break out of rigid academic molds and seek new horizons. The *S.S. Universe* and Semester at Sea seemed the perfect answer for many. For a time-frame that would span three decades, U.S. students and academicians and, increasingly, foreign students and professors would be drawn to the *Universe* and the Semester at Sea program she housed.

In 1981 academic affiliation for Semester at Sea was transferred to the University of Pittsburgh. There international support for the program was broadened further through the university's widely respected Center for International Studies.

Captain Yu-Ren Chang, Master of the Universe and Dr. John Tymitz, Executive Director of the Institute for Shipboard Education.

The common denominator as shipboard education changed academic sponsorship from Chapman College to the University of Colorado to the University of Pittsburgh was the *S.S. Universe*. It was this ship that became the heart and soul of Semester at Sea. And it was this ship for which C.Y. Tung, much like Arnold Bernstein some twenty years earlier, developed a special affection. Tung had gone on to build massive ships—the 564,736 ton supertanker *Seawise Giant*, the 150,000 ton *Energy Transmission*, and the 92,520 ton *Brazilian Friendship*. Yet this old, small, converted cargo ship held a special place in his heart. He visited it often. It was not unlike him to pop in on students in Rio or Manila or Jakarta or elsewhere along the itinerary of a Semester at Sea voyage. He enjoyed the one-on-one contact with students. He delighted in hearing about their on-board classes. He reveled in their excitement in meeting people of diverse cultures. With every visit he became more convinced that the mission of his ship was a vital one, and the role he had carved out for this old liner suited her perfectly.

Those who knew the *Universe* agreed with Tung, Norman Cousins included. In his June 18, 1977 syndicated column he wrote, "If the purpose of education is to prepare an individual for the world beyond the school, then the *S.S. Universe* is superbly attuned to the times."

C.Y. Tung passed away unexpectedly in Hong Kong on April 15, 1982, at the age of seventy. His official funeral was held in Hong Kong. Thousands of people attended the three-day Buddhist ceremony. Memorial services to commemorate his life were also held in New York City and Taiwan. The most fitting and touching of all the services held in his honor were those conducted at sea. Three of his ships were selected to scatter his ashes in the oceans of the world: the *Canadian Explorer* in the Atlantic, the *China Container* in the Indian Ocean, and the *S.S. Universe* in the Pacific.

On a rain-soaked afternoon in the mid-Pacific as the *Universe* was steaming toward Seattle, the entire faculty and student body of the spring 1982 Semester at Sea voyage looked on in silence as Captain Yen committed Tung's ashes to sea from the stern of the ship. The *Universe* then made three complete circles around the burial site before heading back on course. As the students and faculty made their way back to their cabins and classrooms, they talked of this gentle Chinese man who had made such an impact on American education. A short while later Dr. Wesley Posvar, the chancellor of the University of Pittsburgh, also spoke of Tung at a commemorative gathering at the Asia Society in New York:

His experience in shipping imbued him with an awareness of the vast chasms that separate the cultures, the philosophical value systems, the political systems...but he knew there was a remedy. He said that ships carry not only people and goods but they also carry ideas. I think this appreciation for world understanding coupled with Chinese respect... for learning, for scholarship, provided the impetus to his drive for shipboard education. He understood...that the international system of this planet is truly being transformed by new factors of communication and new transnational institutions....He understood even more importantly that there is a world intellectual community with potential for the prevention or at least reduction of international conflict....And finally, he knew that far more than fleets of great ships, education is the essential investment in the future of the world.

With the dominant figure in the life of the *Universe* now gone, there was concern about her future. The concern was quickly put to rest with the receipt of a letter by Dr. Max Brandt, the dean of the spring 1982 voyage. The letter was from C.Y. Tung's eldest son, Chee-Hwa Tung, and said in part: "I do wish to take this opportunity of assuring you and through you to your faculty members and the student body, that although my father has passed away, his special dreams and project of the *Universe* will be carried on with vigor and great efforts. I do hope as time goes on the program will achieve new heights."

Chee-Hwa Tung's letter proved prophetic. The September 1991 voyage of the *S.S. Universe* marks the twentieth year this ship has been sailing as a floating university. The statistics of its twenty years of academic life are staggering: thirty-eight voyages around the world, twenty-two voyages under the academic aegis of the University of Pittsburgh, over three quarters of a million miles traveled, over sixty ports visited, over 2,000 college-level courses offered, and over 17,000 students representing nearly 200 colleges and universities on board.

As the *S.S. Universe* sails into the '90s, it will maintain a twice-a-year schedule of around-the-world Semester at Sea voyages. The ship will continue to serve as dormitory, lecture hall, student union, faculty club, infirmary, gymnasium, and dining hall for these academic adventures. Integrated into each globe circling itinerary will be sixty to seventy University of Pittsburgh accredited courses that range from International Economics to World Literature to Modern Theater to Religion and Culture.

In her twenty years of service as a floating university the *Universe* has seen many additions and changes: a student computer facility, a modernized theater, increased library holdings, added classrooms, an enlarged bookstore, and cellular phone service. Through it all, however, the easy-going, comfortable character of this ship has stayed the same. Life among her decks has not changed much since her initial voyage for Chapman College in 1971.

When faculty and students board the ship confusion reigns. The ship is a strange and congested place. The new passengers feel displaced, apart from one another. As the days flow by—as course work intensifies and port experiences multiply—the ship becomes a sanctuary, a "Great White Mother." At the end of a voyage when the ship approaches the United States, her inhabitants have formed a close, caring community that shares a common bond. For one hundred days they have had the world as a classroom and the *Universe* as a home.

宇宙学府

OF HOMER AND A MODERN-DAY ODYSSEY

Homer's *Odyssey*. Its been called the best story ever written. At the heart of this three-thousand-year-old epic is humanity's ceaseless striving to create a more civilized world in which dignity, reason, and order prevail. The mission of the hero, Odysseus, as he voyages toward home from distant lands, is one of discovery of the world, self-revelation, and learning to live in accordance with this newfound knowledge. Despite loneliness, hardship, exhaustion, and near-overwhelming obstacles, Odysseus exhibits a remarkable capacity for self-preservation. In the course of his lifelong quest to discover his proper relation to the gods and his fellow human beings, he returns home to be reunited with his family.

The parallel between the *Odyssey* and Semester at Sea is inescapable—students on a long voyage learning about themselves and the world, from the world itself.

Traveling in a way that stimulates the intellect, that heightens appreciation for the beauty of the planet and what humanity has accomplished on it, is the major ingredient of this unconventional educational enterprise. And traveling in the Homeric/Semester at Sea sense is to invite reflection and, ultimately, metamorphosis into the experience of one's life. Essayist Lance Morrow says it best:

Travel is always individual and indefinable. It makes the neurons glow in a new way. It excites possibilities. People and scenery mean worlds they cannot mean except when we come to them for the first time as strangers. It is always oneself that one encounters in traveling: other people, of course, other parts of the world, other times carved into stone now overgrown by jungle—but still always oneself.

Semester at Sea is easy to talk about but very difficult to define. One can only paraphrase Franz Werfel in *The Song of Bernadette*, "If you have ever been on Semester at Sea, no explanation is necessary, if you have never been on Semester at Sea, no explanation is possible." Yet one can harken back to the dicta of some of the wisest chroniclers of our times to discover its underlying premises and objectives—to Elbert Hubbard's "A school should not be a preparation for life, a school should be life"; to T.H. White's "Education is experience and the essence of experience is self-reliance"; to Dean Inge's "The world belongs to those who think and act with it, who keep a finger on its pulse"; to Arthur Schopenhaurer's "The world in which a man lives shapes itself chiefly by the way he looks at it"; to Carl Jung's "The world begins to exist when the individual discovers it"; to A.B. Alcott's "Observations more than books, experience rather than persons are the prime educators"; to John Locke's "The only fence against the world is a thorough knowledge of it."

At a minimum one can say Semester at Sea is a process—a process whereby students begin to realize that their culture is *a* culture rather than *the* culture and that human actions can be creatively varied. Americans suffer from indifference and smugness. We are often apathetic and close our minds to genuine understanding of "foreigners" and "foreign ways." Why are we indifferent? Why are we complacent? Paul Fussel in *Citizen Abroad* argues that the answer lies partially in the high value our society places on wealth and material things. Fussel reminds us what Walter Lippman said years ago: "Our prosperity is acting as a narcotic...our public life has been increasingly doped and without purpose. Thus we drift with no one to state our purposes and to make policy...we find ourselves without a chart in very troubled waters."

What Semester at Sea does is sail directly into these troubled waters in an effort to address human destiny, not just geographic destiny. Students return from their voyage knowing that there are vast continents of people far from the shores of the United States who, in their own special way, are seeking the better way of life that all people seek. They return home then, not feeling less American, but with a deeper insight into themselves and a deeper attachment to the world.

In the final analysis, it is what one sees on Semester at Sea that is a key element in this academic adventure. The visual experience becomes part and parcel of the intellectual one. Students come to realize that the true mystery of the world is the visible, not the invisible; that as much can be missed by not looking as not knowing and that, ultimately, perceiving reality is the first step to changing it.

No set of photographs could ever fully describe Semester at Sea. The images on the following pages are merely an attempt to give an overall impression of the experience. They are not organized in the style of a conventional travel diary—departure to final destination. As travel writer Pico Iyer states, "The destination of any journey is not, after all, the last item on the agenda but rather some understanding, however simple or provisional, of what one has seen." The images, therefore, are structured into a series of small essays that reflect the mental and visual itinerary of the students of the *S.S. Universe* while on their once-in-a-lifetime, globe-circling *Odyssey*.

Civilization is a movement and not a condition, a voyage and not a harbor.

Arnold Toynbee

THE SIGHTS

The world is so full of a number of things, I'm sure we should all be as happy as kings.

Robert Louis Stevenson

*Springtime often brings
wildflowers to the grounds of
the Parthenon—the largest Doric
temple ever completed in Greece.*

23

Moscow, U.S.S.R.

On a freezing November afternoon a Russian tour group pauses for a moment in Red Square to have a portrait made.

24

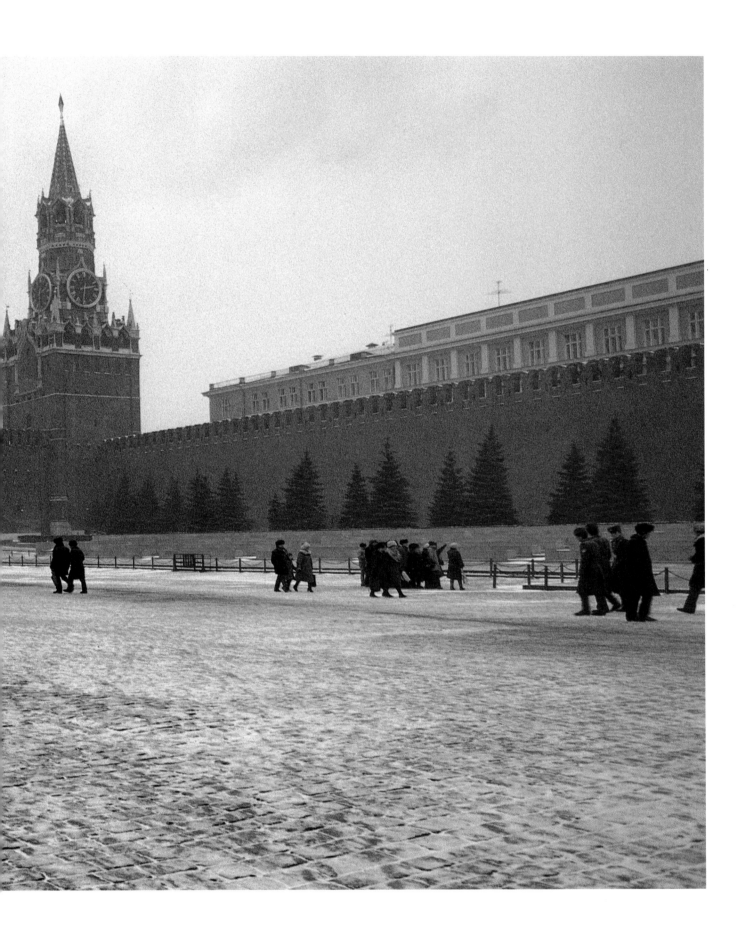

Agra, India

The Taj Mahal at dawn.

Mahabalipuram, India

A man's feet should be planted in his country, but his eyes should survey the world.

George Santayana

Marrakesh, Morocco

Brilliantly colored skeins and cloths hung out to dry are a common sight in the dyers' souk.

Santorini, Greece

One of the most popular of the Greek Cyclades Islands, Santorini is noted for its dramatic volcanic landscape. Sheer black cliffs topped by whitewashed buildings stretch around the cauldron shaped bay that serves the west coast port of the island.

Giza, Egypt

Pyramids at sunrise.

Amboseli National Park, Kenya

Road leading into park.

Ba Da Ling, China

Great Wall of China.

Hong Kong

The skyscrapers along the waterfront of Hong Kong Island provide a modern-day backrop to an old Chinese junk.

32

Kobe, Japan
Fire station.

Mahabalipuram,
India

*Shore Temple
at sunrise.*

Istanbul, Turkey

*Suleymaniye Cami (Mosque of Suleiman
the Magnificent) at sunset.*

Giza, Egypt

Pyramid of Mycerinus at sunset.

Bombay, India

The dhobighat is India's answer to the western laundromat. Here, in the Mahalaxmi area of Bombay, the dhobis (laundry men) and dhobens (laundry women) gather every morning to ply their trade.

Koyasan, Japan

*Slippers are required footware
for all guests of a ryokan
(traditional Japanese inn).*

Mt. Koya, Japan
Mausoleum wall.

Near Kobe, Japan

*A hillside Ujigami Shinto
shrine (small district shrine)
with traditional Torii gate.*

Kyoto, Japan
Kinkaku-ji (Golden Pavilion).

Near Kandy, Sri Lanka

Rice terraces are a predominant feature of the central Sri Lankan hill country.

Guangzhou,
China

*Peasant
attire at the
Wei Ping
Commune.*

Keelung, Taiwan

Advertisement for the Pine and Juniper Art School.

Benares, India

Old wall at the Dasaswamedh Ghat.

*I*t is beauty I seek,
not beautiful things.

Plato

THE PEOPLE

We don't get to know people when they come to us; we must go to them to find out what they are like.

Goethe

Benares, India

A cup of tea and Hatha yoga are daily morning rituals for many who live in this northeastern Indian city.

Keelung, Taiwan
*Morning exercise in
Chungcheng Park.*

Beijing, China
*Morning exercise in
Bei Hai Park.*

Beijing, China

A ninety year-old man begins every day with exercise at the base of the Temple of Heaven in Tiantan Park.

Shanghai, China

The salvation of mankind lies only in making everything the concern of all.

Alexander Solzhenitsyn

Cairo, Egypt

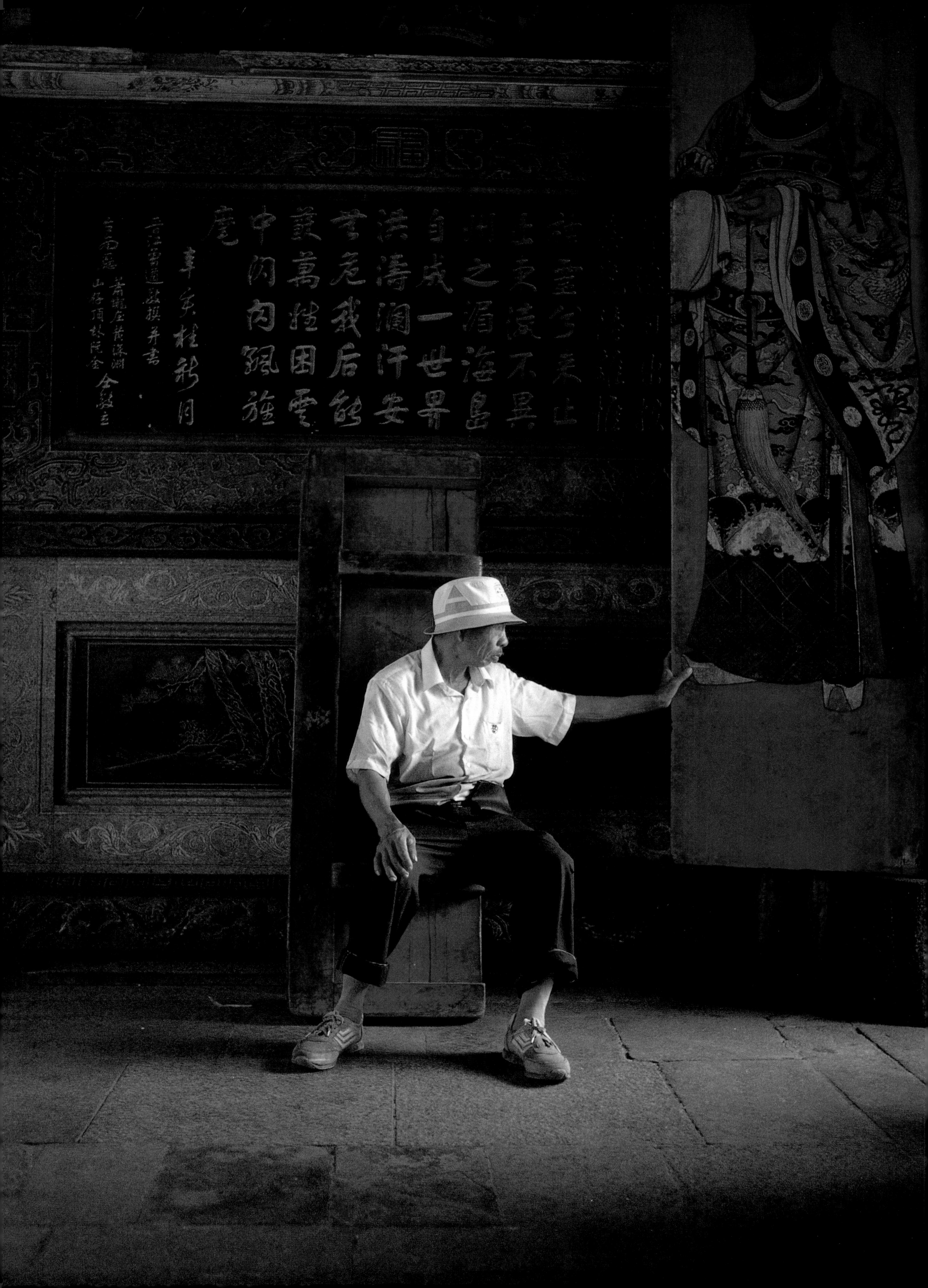

Kyoto, Japan

Guangzhou, China

Lukang, Taiwan

Istanbul, Turkey

Benares, India

A sadhu (holy man) starts the day by watching the sunrise over the Ganga.

Istanbul, Turkey

*A resident of the streets starts
the day by taking stock of
his belongings.*

Marrakech, Morocco

Bombay, India

Tangier, Morocco

Benares, India

61

Beijing, China

*Two old friends enjoy a moment
of solitude as dawn breaks
over the city.*

Marrakech, Morocco

Capetown, South Africa

Fez, Morocco

Marrakech, Morocco

65

Lionshead Mountain, Taiwan

The day begins early for the workers at the Buddhist enclave near Hsinchu in northern Taiwan.

67

Mahabalipuram, India

*A solitary figure strolls
along the beach of the Bay
of Bengal as day breaks
over the dual shrined
Shore Temple.*

*Out of the shadows of night
    The world rolls into light;
It is daybreak everywhere.*

Longfellow

Yangshuo, China

Be it transportation, the irrigation of crops, or the means to do the wash, the Li River plays an important role in the lives of the people.

69

Yangshuo, China

Prior to being taken to market, large baskets keep vegetables cool and fresh in a Li River tributary.

71

Shenzhen, China

A single shirt is all that
remains to dry after a day
of doing the wash.

Bombay, India

La Guaira, Venezuela

Madras, India

Cairo, Egypt

73

Amboseli National Park, Kenya

*Just before the rainy season, a Masai
woman fills in the cracks of her roof
with fresh cow dung. Maintaining the
house, including all weather-proofing,
is the responsibility of the woman
in Masai society.*

Kovacica, Yugoslavia

Usce, Yugoslavia

Pag, Yugoslavia

Istanbul, Turkey

Benares, India

A pilgrim relaxes in a moment of quiet reflection at one of the many stone step ghats that extend along the Ganga and wed the city to the sacred river.

79

Pag, Yugoslavia

Pag, Yugoslavia

Pag, Yugoslavia

Studenica, Yugoslavia

*One of the few remaining monks
in residence at the Serbian
Studenica Monestary.*

81

Lukang, Taiwan

Pec, Yugoslavia

Jakarta, Indonesia

Bombay, India

83

Istanbul, Turkey

Istanbul, Turkey

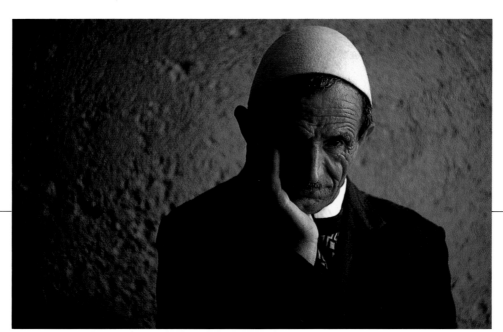

Pec, Yugoslavia

84

Cairo, Egypt

Bombay, India

Lukang, Taiwan

Guangzhou, China

A peasant makes his way home along a small tributary of the Pearl River.

Jakarta, Indonesia

Bahariya, Egypt

Alora, Spain

Two new friends.

Jajce, Yugoslavia
Two old friends.

Bombay, India

Chidambaram, India

Bahariya, Egypt

Keelung, Taiwan

Pusan, Korea

A young schoolboy momentarily loses his balance during a visit to a city park.

Koyasan, Japan
Japanese school girls.

Taipei, Taiwan

Police march in front of the Chiang Kai-shek Memorial Hall as part of "Double-Ten."

Taipei, Taiwan

Students celebrate "Double-Ten".

Taipei, Taiwan

The "Dragon Dance" is an annual rite of the "Double-Ten" celebration—Taiwan's most important national holiday. "Double-Ten" refers to the tenth day of the tenth month and commemorates the overthrow of the Manchu Ching Dynasty on October 10, 1911.

Taipei, Taiwan

Soldiers march in front of the Chiang Kai-shek Memorial Hall as part of "Double-Ten."

Cairo, Egypt
The Khan el-Khalili Bazzar.

Piraeus, Greece
*A street corner
vegetable stand.*

Pusan, Korea
The city fish market.

Keelung, Taiwain
The city market.

Pusan, Korea
Fish market.

Lukang, Taiwan
Hat salesman.

100

Keelung, Taiwan
City market.

Prizren, Yugoslavia
Street vendors.

101

Marrakech, Morocco

*Handwoven rugs are aired-out
on factory rooftops before being
taken to the shops in the Medina.*

Fez, Morocco

*Skins are laid out to dry on a
tannery rooftop.*

Santorini, Greece

A woman draws well water for use in cooking the evening meal.

Shenzhen, China

*When friends visit
from afar, is this not indeed a pleasure?*

Confucius

Pec, Yugoslavia

Pag, Yugoslavia

Sunday afternoon conversation and contemplation in the Trg Bratstva i Jedinstva (central square).

Hong Kong

Kyoto, Japan

Cadiz, Spain

107

Cadiz, Spain

Kosovo Polje, Yugoslavia

Istanbul, Turkey

108

Giza, Egypt

Shanghai, China

Taipei, Taiwan

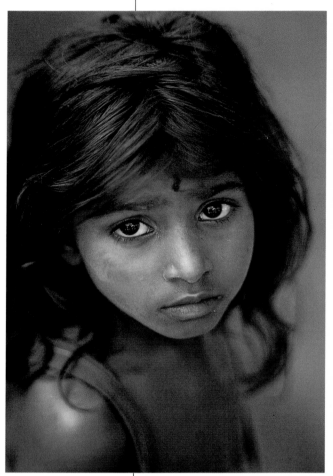

Madras, India

Bombay, India

*C*hildren are poor men's riches.

Proverb

Madras, India

Cairo, Egypt

Guangzhou, China

Bombay, India

Matheran, India

113

The Transkei (South Africa)

Cairo, Egypt

Himeji, Japan

Madras, India

If there is such a thing as civilization, it is because women tend to live a long time.

Roger Rosenblatt

Cairo, Egypt

116

Istanbul, Turkey

Benares, India

117

Chidambaram, India

Keelung, Taiwan

*An American photographer gets
"photographed."*

Kyoto, Japan
Step one.

Kyoto, Japan
Step two.

Cairo, Egypt

Three children in Cairo's Old City enjoy their brief encounter with an American photographer.

123

Anuradhapura, Sri Lanka

Bentota, Sri Lanka

La Guaria, Venezuela

Banaue, Philippines

Athens, Greece

Capetown, South Africa

Bombay, India

Prizren, Yugoslavia

127

Matheran, India

Bombay, India

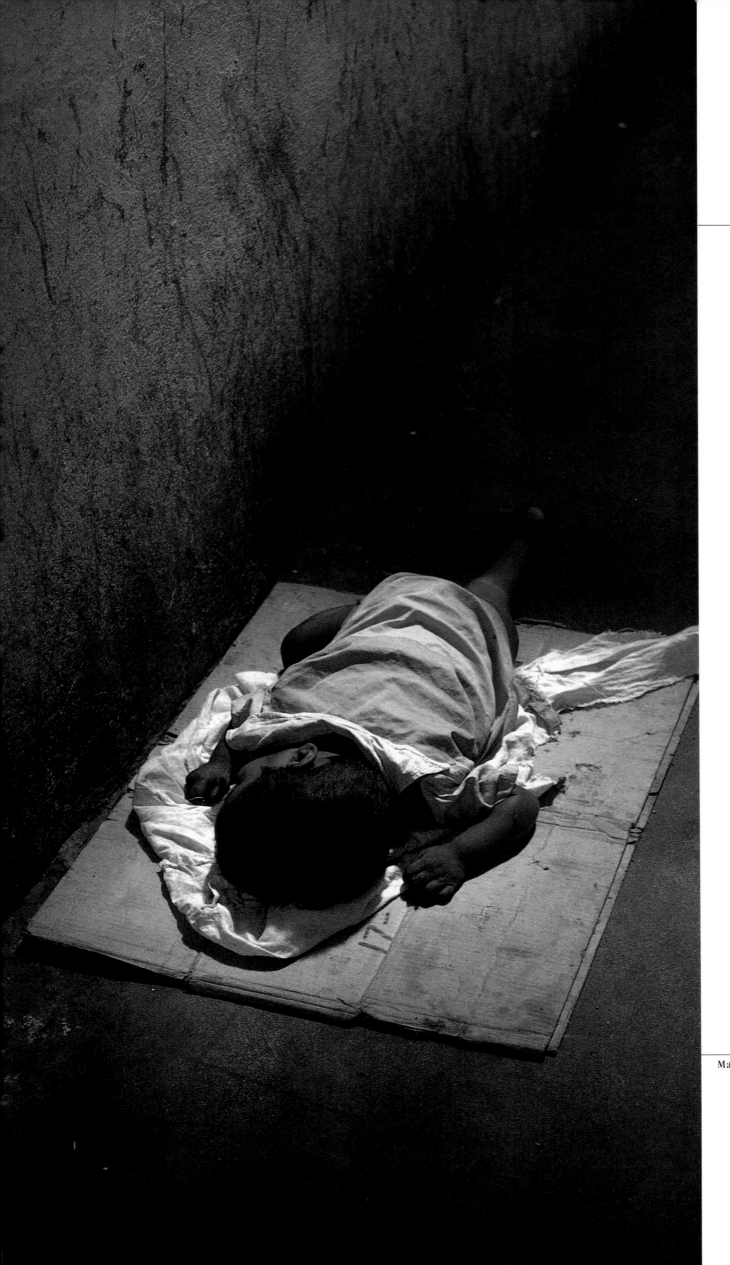

Madras, India

129

Kanchipuram, India

*The early morning sun brings
welcome warmth to two men
who have spent the night in the
chill damp air.*

Kyoto, Japan

Changhua, Taiwan

132

The Transkei (South Africa)

Colombo, Sri Lanka

People have one thing in common:
They are all different.

Robert Zend

THE ANIMALS

A ll animals are equal, but some animals are more equal than others.

George Orwell

Istanbul, Turkey

Benares, India

136

Giza, Egypt

A camel gets some rest after a busy day hauling tourists around the pyramids.

Prizren, Yugoslavia

Cairo, Egypt

139

DRIED
LAVER
PRODUCT OF
KOREA

Pusan, Korea

In an area normally teeming with people, a lone cat is the only customer at this seafood stall near the waterfront.

Amboseli National Park, Kenya
Cattle egret and Cape buffalo.

Kandy, Sri Lanka
Indian elephants.

Amboseli National Park, Kenya
African elephant.

Amboseli National Park, Kenya
Masai giraffe.

Cairo, Egypt

*Morning feeding at
a camel auction.*

Cairo, Egypt

*Hundreds of camels are sold
every week at this auction on
the outskirts of the city.*

Jericho, Israel

Istanbul, Turkey

Istanbul, Turkey

Benares, India

Benares, India

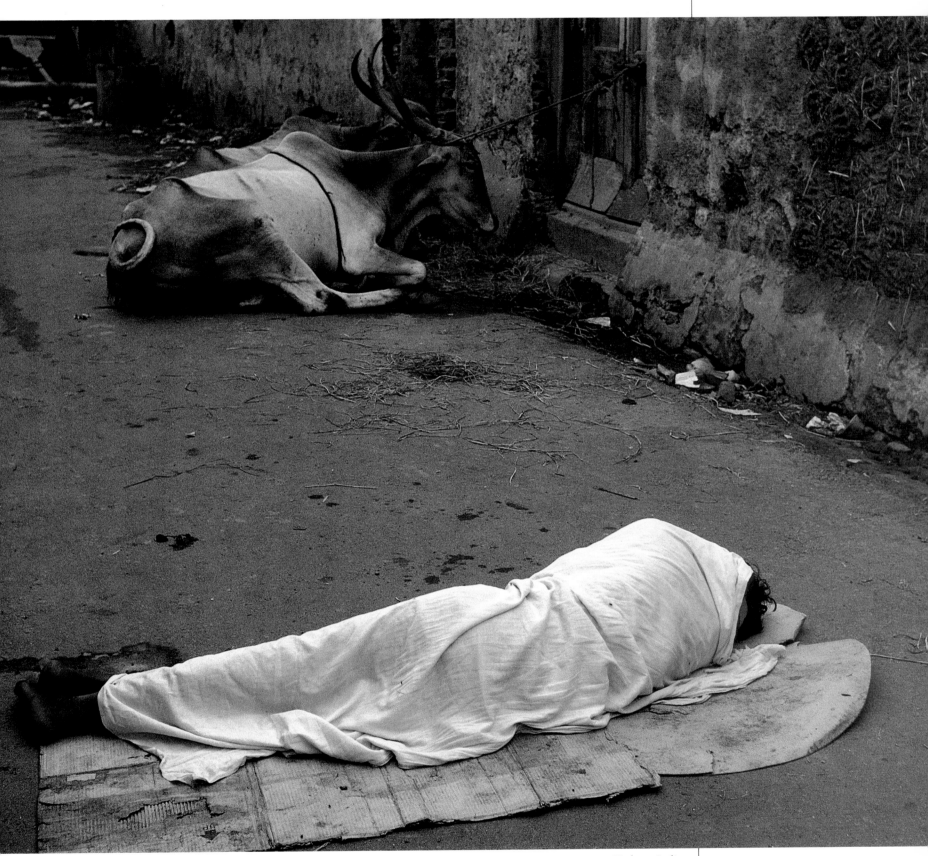

Madras, India

149

Eyup, Turkey

A recent purchase at the Bazzar awaits transport home.

Amboseli National Park, Kenya

With the grasslands around her village barren, a Masai uses a donkey to move the family belongings to better grazing lands.

Fez, Morocco

Donkeys are a primary mode of transportation through the narrow streets of the medina.

151

Giza, Egypt

*A "camel jockey" makes his way
home after a long day of
providing rides for the tourists
who visit the pyramids.*

THE RELIGIONS

There is only one religion, though there are a hundred versions of it.

George Bernard Shaw

Benares, India

*Pilgrims from all over the
subcontinent crowd the sacred
Ganga at sunrise. To them
it is the river of rivers,
"the liquified form of God."*

157

Tien-Hsiang, Taiwan
Cheung Tak Temple.

Kyongju, Korea
Pulguk-sa Temple.

Dubrovnik, Yugoslavia
St. Blaise Church.

Bombay, India
*The symbols of Christianity are
not uncommon sights in this
predominantly Hindu city.*

Cairo, Egypt

*A small group of men participate
in noon prayers at the
Madrassa of Sultan Hassan.
This fourteenth century
complex is one of the world's
largest mosques.*

160

Jerusalem, Israel

Afternoon prayers at the Wailing Wall.

Jerusalem, Israel

Afternoon prayers at the Wailing Wall.

161

Benares, India

*Two sadhus look on as
a man has his head shaved
to signify the recent death of his
mother. This marks the beginning
of the mourning period.*

Benares, India

*Sacred anointment in the
Ganga is a morning rite
practiced by this resident of
the oldest living city on earth.
To Hindus, bathing in the Ganga
is like bathing in heaven.*

165

Kovacica, Yugoslavia

*The Sunday morning sermon
holds the attention of these
Evangelisticka church members.*

Kovacica, Yugoslavia

P*rayer is not an old women's idle* *amusement. Properly understood and applied, it is the most* *potent instrument of action.*

Mohandas Gandhi

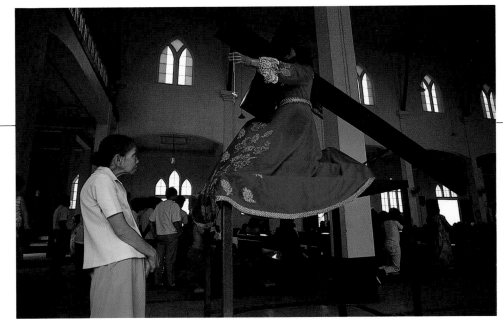

Manila, Philippines
Prayers–Catholic church.

Bombay, India
Prayers–Hindu temple.

Bombay, India
Prayers–Jain temple.

Madras, India
Funeral procession.

Koyasan, Japan

A group of Buddhist monks stands in silence in front of one of the many temples on Mt. Koya.

Taipei, Taiwan

At the Lungshan Temple, Taipei's oldest and most famous Buddhist structure, devotees bring offerings and pray for good fortune and guidance.

173

Kovacica, Yugoslavia

*Confirmation ceremonies
at the Evangelisticka church.*

Jerusalem, Israel

*A rabbinical student passes the
Israeli Army on his way to pray
at the Wailing Wall.*

*R*eligion is the substance of culture,
and culture the form of religion.

Paul Tillich

Benares, India

A sadhu uses the first light of dawn to study his Hindu faith.

Eyup, Turkey

Hundreds of devout Muslims participate daily in noon prayers at the Eyup Sultan Cami (Mosque of The Great Eyup).

Pec, Yugoslavia

A lone man waits for 5:00 o'clock prayers to begin at the Bajrakli Mosque.

177

Polonnaruwa, Sri Lanka

An elderly lady prays in the sacred Buddhist area known as Gal Vehera.

Keelung, Taiwan

A devout Buddhist participates in morning prayers in Chungcheng Park.

Benares, India

A sadhu offers an early morning prayer to the sun.

Kanchipuram, India

A young Hindu pilgrim offers a last minute prayer to Vishnu from her bus window.

Benares, India

Two Brahmins, who will spend the day blessing pilgrims for a small fee, perform their early morning chores at their station on the Ganga.

181

Santorini, Greece
Greek orthodox church.

Changhua, Taiwan

This seventy-two foot statue of Buddha on Pakuashan peak in central Taiwan is the largest Buddha in the country.

Rio de Janeiro, Brazil

The 130 foot statue of Christ on Corcovado (Hunchback) Mountain was originally built as a peace symbol. The outstretched arms serve as a welcome to all travelers.

Nuwara Eliya, Sri Lanka

Once used to signal the arrival of visitors, a bell tower is all that remains of a Hindu temple destroyed in 1983 during the country's civil strife.

THE WORLD OF THE UNIVERSE

If you plan for one year, plant rice. If you plan for ten years, plant trees. If you plan for a hundred years, educate people.

Indian Saying

Vancouver, Canada
Boarding.

Seattle, Washington
Celebrating.

Seattle, Washington
Sorting.

Vancouver, Canada
The odyssey begins.

187

South China Sea

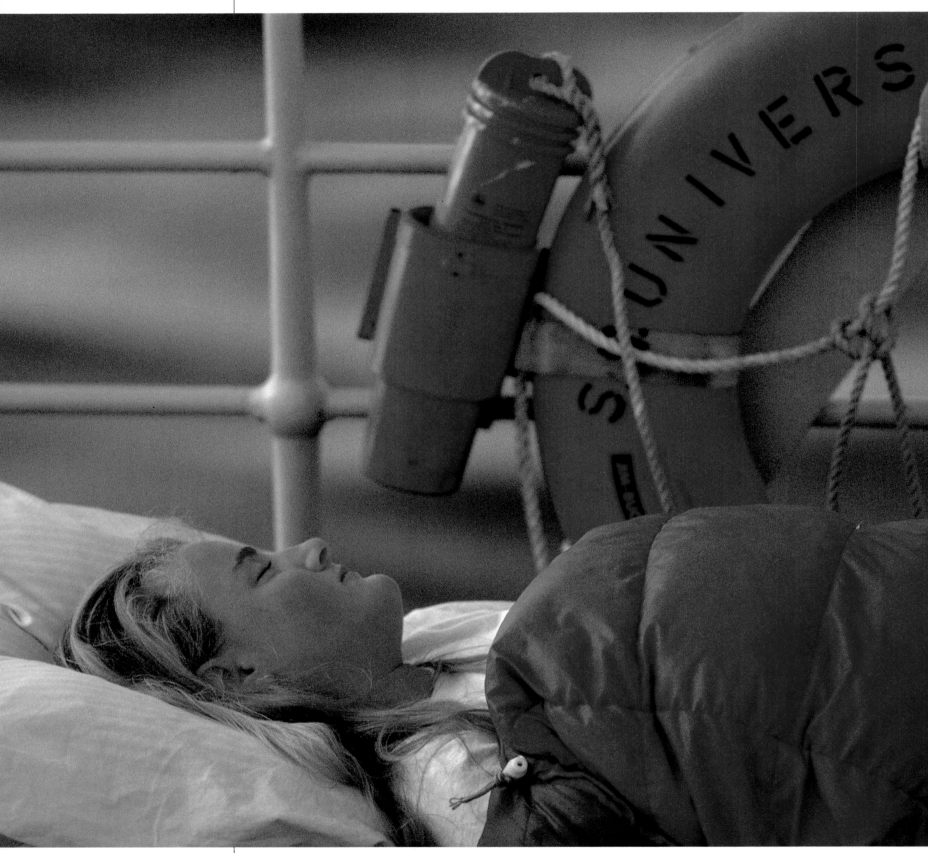

S.S. Universe, Indian Ocean
Dawn.

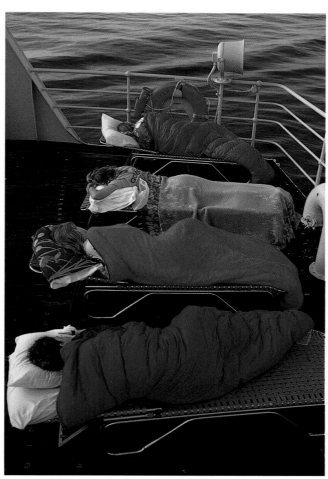

S.S. Universe, Indian Ocean

Just prior to an 8:00 o'clock class.

S.S.Universe, Indian Ocean

*Just prior to a 9:00
o'clock class.*

S.S. Universe
Crew Taijiquan.

194

S.S. Universe

A Sunday at sea.

Hong Kong

Hong Kong

Hong Kong

199

Hong Kong

Jakarta, Indonesia

The use of traveling is to regulate imagination by reality, and instead of thinking how things may be, to see them as they are.

Samuel Johnson

Madras, India
A warm greeting from the S.S. Universe.

Madras, India
A warm welcome from India.

Madras, India

A dock worker proudly displays a gift from an Ivy-Leaguer.

203

Bombay, India

Vancouver, Canada

Madras, India

At Sea

205

S.S. Universe, The Equator
Neptune Day activity.

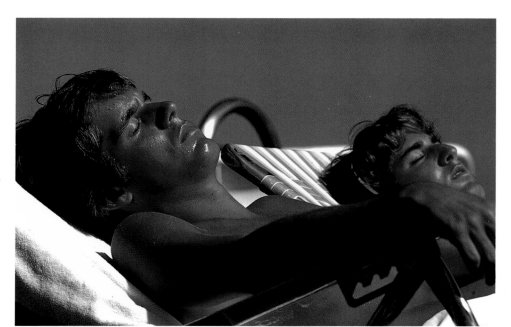

S.S. Universe, The Equator
Post-Neptune Day activity.

S.S. Universe, The Equator
*King Neptune and
Queen Minerva.*

S.S. Universe

*A crew member greets the dawn
in the Atlantic Ocean.*

S.S. Universe
Adriatic Sea.

S.S. Universe
Indian Ocean.

S.S. Universe
Indian Ocean.

S.S. Universe

Sunrise on the volleyball court.

S.S. Universe

Looking back and looking ahead.

S.S. Universe

Early risers.

S.S. Universe
Pacific Ocean.

S.S. Universe
Agean Sea.

S.S. Universe
Indian Ocean.

214

S.S. Universe

Reflecting on an odyssey.

Ft. Lauderdale, Florida
Coming home.

Baltimore, Maryland
Coming home with stuff.

Ft. Lauderdale, Florida
*Farewell to the Universe and
farewell to friends.*

Baltimore, Maryland
Souvenirs.

San Francisco, California
Home.

Ft. Lauderdale, Florida
Home.

Ft. Lauderdale, Florida
One last photograph.

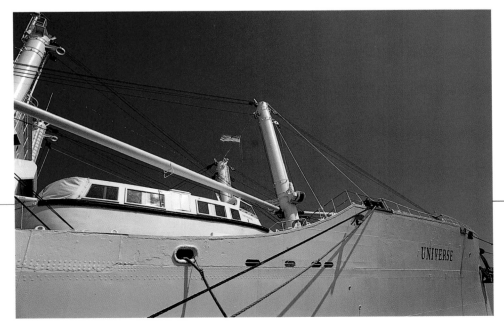

Seattle, Washington
Home.

219

Things do not change; we change.

Thoreau

ACKNOWLEDGMENTS

Authorship of this book is attributed to only one person. However, making *Odyssey* a reality was really the result of contributions and support of many friends, colleagues and shipmates. Sincere appreciation and heartfelt gratitude is extended to all of them. Thank you to typographer Tammy Baker for the innovative and tireless effort on the pre-production phase of this project. Thank you to fellow photographer David Becker for digging up additional material on the *Queen*. Thank you to Brooks Institute student Ricardo Belcher for the many hours spent in the studio copying the historical photographs. Thank you to United States Merchant Marine Academy Chief Librarian Dr. George Billy for the assistance provided in researching *The Story of the Universe*. Thank you to maritime historian Frank Braynard for opening one of the world's most comprehensive archives on ocean liners to a complete stranger. Thank you to Brooks Institute Lab Manager Chris Broughton for solving all the darkroom problems. Thank you to Brooks Institute student Y.K. Cheung for providing the calligraphy to make the *Universe* unquestionably Chinese. Thank you to educator and world traveler Judy Dennehy for the wonderful hospitality and assistance in New York City during embryo phase of the project. Thank you to frequent lunch partners Fran Gordon and Monica Jetton for typing, re-typing, re-typing and re-typing the original manuscript. Thank you to author Robert Lindsey and editor Amy Macionis for the invaluable advice and counsel on the text. Thank you to photojournalist Tomislav Peternek and Brooks Institute student Nino Rakicevic for making photographic life in Yugoslavia an invigorating and stimulating experience. Thank you to William and Allen Publishers Dr. Don Rogers and Judy Rogers for paving the way. Thank you to photographer, designer, and Vice-President for Education at Brooks Institute Mike Verbois for quite simply taking charge of this project and getting it done. Thank you to Ruth Verbois for always being there when needed, keeping Mike in line, and the food.

Finally, special mention must be made of the small group of dedicated and committed individuals who comprise the Institute for Shipboard Education. It is through the efforts of these people that the dream of a Semester at Sea on the *S.S. Universe* comes true for approximately 1000 college students every year. To Chris Asenjo, Julian Asenjo, Max Brandt, Arlette Comunale, Barbara Garvey, Marcia Gruver, Ellen Kolovos, Ozelle Krukowski, Les McCabe, Elizabeth McDermott, Patricia Merlo, Cathy Light, Mary Jo O'Malley, Amy Toner, Thomas Tsui, John Tymitz, Rebecca Walter, Paul Watson and Jill Wright, thank you for keeping the dream alive.

P.L.
Santa Barbara, California
May 1991